FIESTA
FIREWORKS

FIESTA FIREWORKS

GEORGE ANCONA

Lothrop, Lee & Shepard Books 🌀 Morrow
NEW YORK

To Allen and Millie Hart

To those who helped in my explorations of *La Pirotécnica*—

In Tultepec, the people who graciously took part in the project:
Paula Isabel Urbán Gamboa, Leonardo Cortés Ponce, and their son, Alfonso;
Laura Urbán Gamboa, Jesús Reyes Gonzalez, little Laura Caren Reyes Urbán,
and her grandfather, Angel Urbán Sanchez; Silvestre Urbán, Tomas Galván,
and Felipe Cortéz.

In Tepoztlán:
Antonino Villamil Sedano, Emiliano and María Flores Navarrete,
and Valentín Sanchez Castillo.

To those who helped in the research:
Genoveva Rosales López in Oaxaca; Antropólogo Sr. Alejandro Guzmán of
Fonart in Mexico City; Jim Dunlop in Santa Fe, New Mexico;
and Arnold Epstein in Cuernavaca.

¡Gracias!

The text type is 16-point Humanist Slabserif 712.

Published by Lothrop, Lee & Shepard Books
an imprint of Morrow Junior Books
a division of William Morrow and Company, Inc.
1350 Avenue of the Americas, New York, NY 10019
http://www.williammorrow.com

Printed in Singapore at Tien Wah Press.

10 9 8 7 6 5 4 3 2 1

Library of Congress Cataloging-in-Publication Data
Ancona, George.
Fiesta fireworks/George Ancona.
p. cm.
Summary: Describes the preparation of fireworks as well as the
festival honoring San Juan de Dios, the patron saint of Tultepec, Mexico,
which is famous for its master pyrotechnists.
ISBN 0-688-14817-4 (trade)—ISBN 0-688-14818-2 (library)
1. Festivals—Mexico—Tultepec—Juvenile literature.
2. Fireworks—Mexico—Tultepec—Juvenile literature.
[1. Festivals—Mexico. 2. Holidays—Mexico. 3. Fireworks—Mexico.]
I. Title. GT4814.T85A53 1998 394.26972′52—dc21 97-21608 CIP AC

Caren Reyes Urbán lives in Tultepec, Mexico, a town that is famous throughout the country for its fireworks. Today she and her mother are packing a basket of food to take to her grandfather's workshop. *Abuelito* is a master *pirotécnico* (fireworks maker). He makes fireworks that are exploded at *fiestas* all over Mexico.

Caren's father and uncle work with *Abuelito* in his workshop on the outskirts of town. Today they are all too busy to come home for *el almuerzo* (lunch). They are hurrying to finish the fireworks for the *fiesta* honoring Tultepec's patron saint, and they don't have much time—the *fiesta* will begin the day after tomorrow.

When Caren and *Mamá* arrive, *Abuelito* gives Caren a big *abrazo* (hug) and she kisses his scratchy unshaven cheek. *"Hola, m'hijita,"* he says. "Hi, sweetie." Then, with a twinkle in his eye, he adds, "I'm starving!"

Caren and her mother set the table in the shade of a tree. Then they all sit down to eat tacos of *nopalito* (small cactus leaves).

When they finish, Caren and *Mamá* gather the dishes while the men go back to work. *Papá* ties rockets onto a wheel that will go on the *castillo* (castle) they will build in the plaza. *Tío* Leonardo makes a *torito* (little bull). He covers a bamboo frame with paper soaked in a flour paste. After it dries, he will paint it white. Tomorrow it will be decorated and the fireworks will be added.

At home Caren and *Mamá* make a small *torito* for Caren to carry in the parade. Small *toritos* have no fireworks. Many *pirotécnicos* make small *toritos* and *castillos* to sell to visitors as souvenirs.

The next day *tío* Leonardo brings the *toritos* to a neighbor's yard in the *barrio* (neighborhood) to be finished. The men of the *barrio* gather to paint the eyes and mouths on the *toritos.* Then they build a bamboo framework on top of each bull to hold the fireworks. They finish by attaching wheels of rockets to the horns and sides.

This year Caren's *barrio* also made a puppet of a bull's head. As soon as it is painted, little Carlitos tries it out, dancing around the yard and making everyone laugh.

The next morning the *fiesta* begins with roosters crowing, church bells ringing, and rockets exploding. Today the town of Tultepec is celebrating its patron saint, San Juan de Dios, protector of *pirotécnicos.*

The front of the church is decorated with the saint's image surrounded by floral designs. Around the church garden, a carpet of colored sawdust is sprinkled on the walk. A procession will carry the saint's statue over the sawdust carpet. Then the smudged dust will be swept away.

Across the street in the plaza, men are already shooting off crackling firecrackers and whooshing rockets. In the midst of the smoke and noise, *Abuelito*'s workers are assembling their *castillo.* Each master *pirotécnico* in Tultepec is building one, and several towers rise high into the sky.

In the afternoon *toritos* and puppets of every size, shape, and color emerge from the houses and yards of the town. A band leads the merry crowd as it moves around Tultepec, gathering more and more *toritos*. With her little *torito* on her head, Caren scurries off to join her friends and neighbors.

Each *barrio* tries to outdo the others with the most fantastic sculptures they can make. Some are so big they have to be carried or pushed by teams of young men.

As the afternoon turns to night, the statue of San
Juan de Dios is carried in a procession around the
church garden, accompanied by church bells and the
explosions of rockets and fireworks. Children carry
giant sparklers. Men carry poles with spinning wheels
of whistling rockets that shoot up into the night sky,
bursting into colorful flowers.

When the procession in the churchyard ends, the parade of *toritos* arrives in the plaza. First the smaller *toritos*, carried by teenage boys, are lit, and bursts of fireworks light up the plaza. The boys charge the cheering crowds, sending whistling *buscapiés* (ground spinners) skittering between their feet.

Next the giant *toros* (bulls) are lit. Bands play and crowds shout and laugh as firecrackers and rockets fill the plaza with colorful fire and smoke.

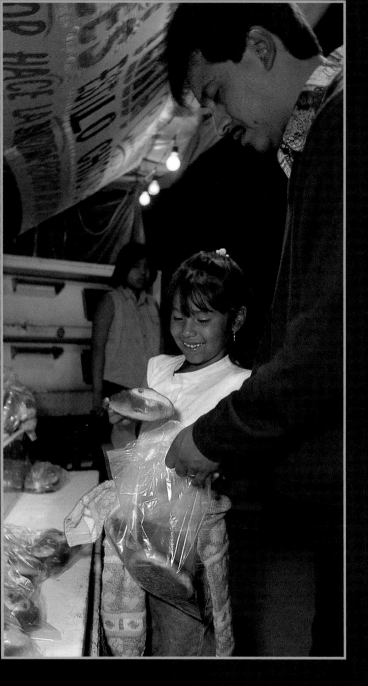

At last the air clears and the crowds move on to the
amusement rides and food stands. *Papá* buys Caren a

Suddenly rockets whoosh skyward, exploding into clusters of swirling stars. It's time for the burning of the *castillos*!

One by one the *castillos* are lit. Their wheels of rockets begin to spin and whistle. On the towers crackling lines of fire trace flowers and moving

Caren holds her ears as she watches *Abuelito* light
the fuse of his *castillo*. A flame sizzles, then explodes
into a bouquet of fire. The wheels spin wildly, sending
rockets into the night sky. "Aaaahhhh!" cries the crowd
as the sky is filled with beautiful explosions. When the
last *castillo* is burned, the crowd bursts into applause.

Caren yawns. It is way past her bedtime. *Papá* lifts her up, and as they make their way through the dark streets, Caren falls fast asleep. That night she will dream of her *torito* and *Abuelito*'s beautiful flowers of fire in the sky. It has been a wonderful *fiesta*.

Author's Note

Fireworks were invented in China and brought to Mexico by the Spanish. Every town in Mexico has a patron saint who is honored annually with a *fiesta*. And almost every *fiesta* has fireworks.

The town of Tultepec is famous for its master pyrotechnists. Almost everyone in town works at making fireworks, which are shipped all over the country.

San Juan de Dios, the patron saint of Tultepec, was a Portuguese monk born in 1495. He miraculously entered a burning hospital many times to save the patients who were trapped inside. The pyrotechnists of Tultepec pray to him for protection in their dangerous work.

Glossary

abrazo *(ah-BRAH-soh)* — hug

abuelito *(ah-bway-LEE-toh)* — little grandfather; an endearment

almuerzo *(al-MWAIR-soh)* — lunch

barrio *(BAH-ree-oh)* — neighborhood

buscapiés *(BOO-skah-pee-AYS)* — ground spinners; fireworks that spin along the ground

castillo *(kahs-TEE-lyoh)* — castle

fiesta *(fee-ESS-tah)* — festival, celebration

hola *(OH-luh)* — hi

m'hijita *(mee-HEE-tuh)* — sweetie; literally, my little daughter; an endearment

nopalito *(noh-pah-LEE-toh)* — small cactus leaf

pan dulce *(pahn DOOL-seh)* — sweet bun

pirotécnico *(pee-roh-TEHK-nee-koh)* — pyrotechnist; fireworks maker

San Juan de Dios *(sahn hoo-AHN deh dee-OHS)* — Saint John of God, patron saint of Tultepec

tío — uncle

torito *(toh-REE-toh)* — little bull

toro *(TOH-roh)* — bull